VERSUS!

Cheetah vs. Tortoise

Eric Braun

BLACK
RABBIT
BOOKS

Hi Jinx is published by Black Rabbit Books
P.O. Box 3263, Mankato, Minnesota, 56002.
www.blackrabbitbooks.com
Copyright © 2018 Black Rabbit Books

Jennifer Besel, editor; Michael Sellner, designer;
Catherine Cates, production designer;
Omay Ayres, photo researcher

Library of Congress Cataloging-in-Publication Data
Names: Braun, Eric, 1971- author.
Title: Cheetah vs. tortoise / by Eric Braun.
Other titles: Cheetah versus tortoise
Description: Mankato, Minnesota : Black Rabbit Books, [2018] |
Series: Hi jinx. Versus! | Audience: Ages 9-12. | Audience:
Grades 4 to 6. | Includes bibliographical references and index.
Identifiers: LCCN 2017009968 (print) | LCCN 2017021635
(ebook) | ISBN 9781680723762 (e-book) |
ISBN 9781680723465 (library binding)|
ISBN 9781680726527 (paperback)
Subjects: LCSH: Cheetah--Juvenile literature. | Testudinidae--
Juvenile literature. | Animals--Miscellanea--Juvenile literature.
Classification: LCC QL737.C23 (ebook) |
LCC QL737.C23 B727 2018 (print) | DDC 590.2--dc23
LC record available at https://lccn.loc.gov/2017009968

Printed in China. 9/17

Image Credits

Contents

Chapter 1
Speed Meets Toughness

Look at these two animals. They're so different! The cheetah is fast. It is exciting. The tortoise is slow. Watching paint dry might be more **thrilling**.

The cheetah would easily win a matchup, right? Actually, it might be closer than you think. The tortoise may be slow. But it's also tough as math. It has a few tricks up its shell too. Who would win?

Chapter 2
Comparing Their Features

Just how fast are cheetahs? Buckle your seatbelt. In short bursts, they can reach 70 miles (113 kilometers) per hour. Cheetahs can easily make sharp turns at high speeds too.

The tortoise? It goes about 26 feet (8 meters) per minute. The world's fastest tortoise once went about 55 feet (17 m) per minute. That's only .6 mile (1 km) per hour!

A cheetah's long, heavy tail helps it make quick turns. The tail's weight provides balance.

Weight

Tortoises come in many sizes. Some are tiny. Others are huge. The Galápagos is one of the largest species. It can reach 550 pounds (249 kilograms). That's more than five times heavier than a toilet!

Compared to other big cats, cheetahs are small. They weigh 77 to 143 pounds (35 to 65 kg).

About That Mouth

Cheetahs run over their **prey**. Then they sink their teeth into the preys' necks. These bites **suffocate** prey.

Tortoises, on the other hand, don't like fast food. And they don't have teeth. Instead, they have powerful beaks. They use them to tear into leaves and veggies. Their mouths have rough edges. The edges can act like teeth.

Special Attack

Cheetahs can't roar. But they can chirp. The sound is similar to that a bird makes. Some people think cheetahs chirp to **lure** birds toward them. Talk about speedy and sneaky!

Tortoises have gular horns on their lower shells. Tortoises use them during fights. They try to flip other tortoises upside down with them. Upside-down tortoises can't attack.

Defense

Cheetahs have great eyesight. They can see **threats** up to 3 miles (5 km) away. When they spot one, they speed away.

Tortoises aren't fast enough to run away. But they don't need to. Tortoises simply hide inside their shells. About 60 bones make up a shell. Strong **keratin** plates cover it.

Most cheetahs live 10 to 12 years. Some tortoises can live more than 100 years.

16

Taking a Time-Out

Cheetahs tire from chasing prey. They have to rest for nearly 30 minutes before eating. Cheetahs aren't safe during this time. They are too tired to fight.

Tortoises spend a lot of time resting. A Galápagos naps for nearly 16 hours every day. Because of its size and shell, it is in little danger.

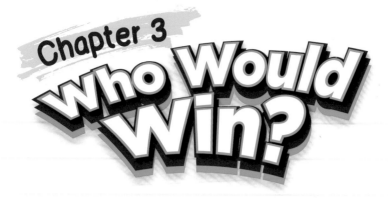

Chapter 3
Who Would Win?

We know the cheetah would win a footrace. But who would win a fight?

Tortoises weigh up to 550 pounds (249 kg). They have strong beaks. They can easily protect themselves.

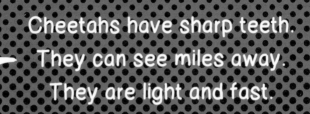

Cheetahs have sharp teeth.
They can see miles away.
They are light and fast.

Chapter 4
Get in on the Hi Jinx

Tortoises may be **sturdy**. But many species are **endangered**. Ploughshare tortoises live in Madagascar. **Poachers** take the animals. They sell them as pets. There are fewer than 600 left in the wild.

To help the species, a team of people breeds the tortoises. They then release the animals into the wild. But before they do, they scratch letters into their shells. The team hopes tortoises with marked shells won't be taken.

Take It One Step More

1. Why do you think tortoises live so long?

2. Would you rather be fast and dangerous or slow and sheltered? Why?

3. What can people learn from tortoises? What about from cheetahs?

GLOSSARY

endangered (in-DAYN-jurd)—close to becoming extinct

keratin (KER-uh-tin)—a protein that makes up hair and horny tissues, such as fingernails

lure (LUHR)—to attract someone or something to an area

poacher (POH-cher)—someone who kills or takes wild animals illegally

prey (PRAY)—an animal hunted or killed for food

sturdy (STUR-dee)—strong and healthy

suffocate (SUHF-uh-kayt)—to kill someone or something by making breathing impossible

threat (THRET)—something that can do harm

thrill (THRIL)—to cause someone to feel very excited or happy

BOOKS

Atlantic, Leonard. *100-Year-Old Tortoises!* World's Longest-Living Animals. New York: Gareth Stevens Publishing, 2017.

Gagne, Tammy. *Giant Galápagos Tortoise.* Back from Near Extinction. Minneapolis: Core Library, an imprint of Abdo Publishing, 2017.

Reinke, Beth Bence. *The Challenging Lives of Cheetahs.* Stories from the Wild Animal Kingdom. Mankato, MN: Child's World, 2018.

WEBSITES

Cheetah Facts for Kids
cheetah.org/about-the-cheetah/for-kids/

Galápagos Tortoise
kids.sandiegozoo.org/animals/galapagos-tortoise

Helping Cheetahs Win the Race to Survive
kids.nationalgeographic.com/explore/nature/cheetahs-race-to-survive/

INDEX